THE CHEAP GUIDE TO SUSTAINABILITY
AND
CORPORATE SOCIAL RESPONSIBILITY

LEO RAUDYS

Printed in the United States of America

First Edition

ISBN 978-0692723333

CONTENTS

Acknowledgements

Many thanks to my reviewers who were invaluable in helping me pull this book together and making sure I got my facts right. All are dear friends who have helped me out numerous times throughout my career. Bridget Croke of the Closed Loop Fund is a business development dynamo and is the best I've ever met (and I've met a lot of them). She's also a fearless rock climber, which, come to think of it, is sort of a metaphor for business development. Scott Weislow is an excellent strategist, one of the hardest workers I've ever encountered and is my go-to person on global product compliance and electronics recycling. Scot Case is an outstanding entrepreneur and green labeling expert and is the person I call whenever I have a question about greenwashing. To all of you, I am in your debt.

Introduction

Welcome to the first edition of *The Cheap Guide to Sustainability and Corporate Social Responsibility.* I wrote this book to serve as a resource for anybody trying to navigate the somewhat convoluted world of sustainability and CSR. It's a complicated landscape filled with acronyms and abbreviations (see, I just used one) that confounds even the most experienced practitioner. Whether you're just getting into the field, are a seasoned pro, or even an outside agitator trying to make life miserable for the rest of us, you should find this guide useful. With any luck, you'll have a better understanding of who's who and what's what, so that at minimum, you can do a better job of explaining to your loved ones exactly what you do, or want to do, for a living.

This guide describes conferences, organizations and many of the players who make up the sustainability universe. You'll also find lists of terms, acronyms and abbreviations that are particularly handy for webinars and conference calls because you can get smart fast without anybody knowing you're looking things up.

This is the first edition, so it's incomplete. If you find something missing, please let me know what you think should be included. There will be subsequent editions, so consider this your opportunity to continue to make the world a better place. And the guide won't cost you any more than a latte. Literally. The price of the book is pegged to the cost of a large latte at Starbucks. If the price of the book goes up, blame Howard Schultz, not me. Anyhow, it's the journey not the destination that matters and it'll likely be a few editions till I start to get this right.

You'll be able to quickly and easily navigate to content using the many links sprinkled throughout the document. If you prefer hardcopy, you won't get the benefit of the links, but you'll be able to put it in your pocket, purse, murse, briefcase or backpack and use it when your phone battery died from too much texting at a conference. The paperback version also has a few pages in the back where you can record your field observations of sustainability people in their natural habitats.

Finally, most of what you'll find here is focused on the United States. It's a big world out there, and I will expand to include more international content as time goes on.

Issues and Trends

Here's a highly abbreviated selection of ideas and terms you'll encounter in the world of sustainability and CSR. It is by no means meant to be inclusive of all of the big issues we're all dealing with - far from it. Consider it a good start.

Circular Economy

The notion that, in a world of finite resources, the only truly sustainable economy is one in which resources are infinitely reused for some other purpose, whether it be through sharing, reuse or recycling. That's the "circular" part. It begins with the business model and product design phase to ensure circularity throughout the life of a product and its packaging. This is different from a linear economy, where things are designed, intentionally or unintentionally, to end up as waste. Entropy being what it is, we may never reach a state of a fully circular economy. However, getting off the linear economy path so that economic growth is decoupled from waste? That would be a really good thing.

Corporate Social Responsibility (CSR)

The concept that businesses can contribute to improving the world through various forms of social and environmental action. Definitions and philosophies of what constitutes CSR are all over the map. People have been arguing about the definition of CSR for years, which is a bit of a time-waster. It's far better to just focus on making things happen and leave the definitional wars behind us.

Creating Shared Value (CSV)

CSV is an alternative (though some say it's merely a modification - there's that definition thing again) to traditional CSR or related models, such as cause marketing. The main idea behind CSV is that a business can generate incremental value or wealth by placing social and environmental issues at the core of its overall business strategy. One example that's cited often is the flooring company Interface. Once upon a time, the company's founder, the late Ray Anderson, had an epiphany of sorts and decided to fundamentally restructure his company around circular economy principles. As a result, carpet recycling isn't an add-on at Interface. It's at the core of what they offer their customers. The change in strategy resulted in company growth and lower social and environmental impacts from their products.

Environmental, Social and Governance (ESG)

Investor-speak for measuring the triple bottom line performance of companies as a way of better evaluating risk and return. It is often confused with socially responsible investing (SRI). The objective of SRI is to generate better returns by investing in companies that meet or exceed high standards of environmental and social performance. And while ESG criteria can be used to evaluate and invest in companies with outstanding environmental and social practices they can also be used to evaluate companies that some people consider to be morally reprehensible. Presumably, the latter companies would fare poorly when rated on ESG factors and would be considered to be riskier investments.

Extended Producer Responsibility (EPR)

EPR is a common business practice in some parts of the world, most notably Europe and Canada. It exists as regulatory policy for a few categories of consumer goods in a smattering of jurisdictions in the U.S. The concept is simple: If you make a product, the cost of recycling and disposal should be borne by you and not society at large. Some manufacturers feel that EPR policies are fundamentally unfair, yet others embrace them. In a world where manufacturers often control many aspects of products we own (think of smart phones and restrictions on your ability to fix them on your own), it's becoming harder to argue that a manufacturer's responsibility for its product doesn't extend beyond the point of sale.

Materiality Assessment

Finding out what really matters to your business as it relates to your impact on the world. Addressing deforestation is material to an agricultural products company. Donating funds to a local school is a very good thing to do, but it's not material. It's ok, actually fantastic, to be able to do both.

Natural Capital

The sum total of the planet's finite natural resources. Explicitly accounting for natural capital is one way of putting a value on externalities in economic analysis. Natural capital includes the geology, soils, air, water and all living organisms on Earth. The concept is fairly straightforward. However, putting a monetary value on natural capital is tricky and fraught with disagreement. Nevertheless, when natural capital or ecosystem services are not accounted for, they are essentially treated as if they're free. And we all know what happens to free stuff. Eventually it's all gone.

Networking

This is about getting to know people. Getting a job or a business deal are outcomes, but they are not networking.

Helping someone get a leg up or get a job, and taking the time to learn about each other's worlds is networking. Calling someone only when you need something is a perfectly fine thing to do, but don't confuse it with networking.

Purpose

A term being used in CSR quite a lot these days to generally convey the notion that people are happier and more engaged in work and life when there is meaning associated with the things that we do. First made popular by the hit TV series *My Name is Earl*, wherein the main character Earl Hickey and his brother Randy engage in ongoing philosophical discussions on purpose, describing it as a reason to wake up every morning and likening it to a box of powdered donut holes. Like most of us, it's not clear if Earl and Randy ever find their purpose, which serves to highlight the notion that the journey is more important than the destination.

Responsibility

Do unto others as you would have them do unto you. Loosely translated, if all you do in your CSR efforts is philanthropy, but your business model results in harm to people and the environment, you have work to do. A lot.

Sustainability

People, Planet, Profit. Triple Bottom Line. Pick whatever slogan or term you like, but the concept is simple: If we don't account for the needs of people and the environment, while fostering economic well-being, the planet is screwed, which means we're screwed.

Transparency

An organization that is meeting its legal requirements to disclose information or highlighting successes is not considered to be a paragon of transparency. Disclosing mistakes, failures and uncomfortable truths when not required to do so, is. Think of the time you asked a family member for a loan and you had to explain you were short of cash because you made too many impulse purchases on QVC. That's what transparency feels like. It's *supposed* to be a little uncomfortable.

Organizations

This is the part of the guide where you can find descriptions of organizations focused on sustainability and CSR. It's an incomplete list and is dominated by NGOs, but again, it's a good start. The information provided is a quick summary of what these organizations do. For details, visit their websites.

Where an organization is known by its acronym or abbreviation, it's included. With any luck, there's an organization in here you've never heard of. As the real estate agents say, all information is deemed reliable but not guaranteed.

Multi-sector/issue Organizations

Association for the Advancement of Sustainability in Higher Education (AASHE)
www.aashe.org
Membership organization dedicated to advancing sustainable innovation in academia.

As You Sow
www.asyousow.org
Organization that promotes corporate environmental and social responsibility through shareholder advocacy and partnerships. Familiar to many people who work in investor relations departments.

B Lab

www.bcorporation.net

NGO dedicated to advancing the idea that businesses have the power to solve social and environmental problems. Operates a program to certify B Corporations, which is a form of incorporation that explicitly expands the purpose of an organization beyond just maximizing shareholder value to include stakeholders and environmental and social issues.

Business for Social Responsibility (BSR)

www.bsr.org

Quite possibly the longest running CSR organization. BSR has extensive expertise in a number of industries. Particularly notable has been their eagerness to work with companies that have significant sustainability challenges, such as those in the extractive industries.

Ceres

www.ceres.org

Sustainability advocacy organization with an emphasis (though not exclusively) on leveraging the power of investment to create a more sustainable economy. Ceres has been very active on climate change, particularly through its BICEP initiative. Helped create the Global Reporting Initiative (GRI).

Environmental Council of the States (ECOS)

www.ecos.org

Association of state environmental agency commissioners. An important part of the environmental policymaking process that tends to operate under the radar.

Environmental Defense Fund (EDF)

www.edf.org

Science-based, non-partisan environmental organization that has made a name for itself as a solid corporate partner. EDF's Climate Corps program has been instrumental in helping many companies cost effectively reduce their carbon emissions.

Environmental Protection Agency (EPA)

www3.epa.gov

Federal agency responsible for creating and implementing environmental regulations. Operates many voluntary programs. Also a significant contributor to environmental science.

Future 500

www.future500.org

An organization committed to bringing diverse stakeholders together to solve big problems. Particularly adept at bringing NGOs and corporations together for productive dialogues.

Global Citizen

www.globalcitizen.org

Global NGO focused on fostering grassroots engagement on big challenges such as sustainability, poverty and inequality. Impressive mobilization efforts, particularly among millennials.

Global Environmental Management Initiative (GEMI)

http://gemi.org

Organization of participating companies dedicated to improving the performance of environmental sustainability programs, with a focus on EHSS programs.

Global Impact Investing Network (GIIN)

www.giin.org

Membership-based NGO dedicated to increasing the scale and effectiveness of impact investing. Excellent resource for networking. Operates exceptional educational programs for people in the investment community and those who support them.

Global Reporting Initiative (GRI)

www.globalreporting.org

International organization that works with stakeholders to set standards for sustainability and CSR reporting.

Greenpeace

www.greenpeace.org

Global environmental advocate with an emphasis on campaigns and direct action to achieve their desired goals.

National Association for Environmental Management (NAEM)

www.naem.org

Networking and educational association for environmental management professionals. Tends to focus on EHSS issues.

Natural Resources Defense Council (NRDC)

www.nrdc.org

The environment's legal team.

Net Impact

www.netimpact.org

Bills itself as "The world's best training ground for the next generation of change agents." The best professional development organization for sustainability at all career stages, though they emphasize working with those who are early in their careers. The annual conference is a great place to meet sustainability-minded MBAs and other students. Hundreds of chapters everywhere. If there isn't one in your neighborhood, start one.

Shared Value Initiative

www.sharedvalue.org
An organization dedicated to fostering the adoption of business practices focused on the concept of shared value.

Sierra Club

www.sierraclub.org
Grassroots environmental advocacy organization founded in 1892 by the legendary environmentalist John Muir. Very active at the local level through dozens of local chapters, each with their own personality.

Sustainability Accounting Standards Board (SASB)

www.sasb.org
Standards setting organization focused on creating accounting standards for ESG reporting. Modeled on traditional accounting standards.

Sustainability Consortium

www.sustainabilityconsortium.org
Founded by Walmart in collaboration with Arizona State University and the University of Arkansas to advance supply chain sustainability throughout the economy. Now a multi-faceted, global organization with a large corporate membership base. Manages the Sustainability Index among a number of other initiatives.

2030 Districts

www.2030districts.org
Grassroots organization dedicated to significantly improving the environmental performance of buildings through public/private collaborations in a number of

major metropolitan areas. Major emphases are energy, water and vehicle emissions associated with commercial properties. Currently, there are twelve districts across the United States and Canada.

US Green Building Council (USGBC)

www.usgbc.org
Membership-based non-profit focused on promoting sustainability in the built environment. Owns and operates the LEED certification program.

World Environment Center

www.wec.org
Global sustainable development organization that works to share and build sustainable development capabilities with member companies.

Climate and Energy

Advanced Energy Economy (AEE)

www.aee.net
National association of leaders involved in some aspect of the energy industry, focused on making the system more secure, clean and affordable.

American Council for an Energy-Efficient Economy (ACEEE)

www.aceee.org
Respected opinion leader focused on improving energy efficiency in the U.S. through education, policy analysis and collaboration with a variety of partners. Hosts a number of excellent workshops and conferences throughout the year.

Association of Climate Change Officers (ACCO)

www.accoonline.org

Member-based organization dedicated to improving organizational leadership practices for people working on climate change.

CDP (Formerly known as Carbon Disclosure Project)

www.cdp.net

Investor-based organization focused on increasing transparency of climate, forest, supply chain and water risks faced by companies, and encouraging reductions of those risks.

Center for Climate and Energy Solutions (C2ES)

www.c2es.org

Formerly known as the Pew Center on Global Climate Change, C2ES is a non-partisan organization working to advance strong policy and action to address climate change.

Climate Counts

www.climatecounts.org

A collaborative effort to bring consumers and companies together to address climate change. Climate Counts issues a scorecard that evaluates the performance and commitment of companies working to reduce their impact on the Earth's climate.

The Climate Group

www.theclimategroup.org

Global NGO whose goal is to help leaders transition to a prosperous low carbon economy. Driven by an optimistic philosophy that a cleaner energy future will create greater opportunity for many sectors of society. Excellent collaborator that has incubated a number of impressive initiatives.

The Climate Registry (TCR)
www.theclimateregistry.org
An interesting and influential public/private sector hybrid that facilitates voluntary and mandatory measuring, reporting and verification of carbon emissions.

Edison Electric Institute (EEI)
www.eei.org
Member-based association that represents all investor-owned electric utilities in the U.S. EEI is a valued resource for energy management practitioners who are looking to keep up with developments in the utility industry.

Investor Network on Climate Risk (INCR)
www.ceres.org/investor-network/incr
A project of Ceres that is a network of over 100 institutional investors representing more than $13 trillion in assets working on addressing the risks and capitalizing on opportunities resulting from climate change and other sustainability challenges.

National Association of Regulatory Utility Commissioners (NARUC)
www.naruc.org
Member-based non-profit representing state public service commissions. Public utility commissions have significant authority and influence over renewable energy projects and energy efficiency programs. NARUC is a key player on those and other areas of utility regulation at the state and local levels.

National Center for Atmospheric Research (NCAR)

https://ncar.ucar.edu
Federally funded research and development organization dedicated to understanding the behavior of the atmosphere. Leading research institution on climate science. Sponsored by the National Science Foundation. Biking the road up to the NCAR headquarters is a great thing to do while in Boulder.

National Renewable Energy Laboratory (NREL)

www.nrel.gov
Major Federal government research institution focused on clean energy innovation.

Rocky Mountain Institute (RMI)

www.rmi.org
Independent, non-partisan organization that is advancing innovations in energy efficiency and renewables. Operates the Business Renewables Center, which helps corporations navigate renewable energy procurement.

350.org

http://350.org
Grassroots climate change movement focused on reducing the concentration of CO_2 in the atmosphere to less than 350 ppm.

We Mean Business

www.wemeanbusinesscoalition.org
Coalition of NGOs, businesses and investors working to accelerate the transition to a low carbon economy.

World Resources Institute (WRI)
www.wri.org
Global research organization that is a key resource for governments, businesses and NGOs on natural resource issues, most notably climate change, forest management and water risk.

Circular Economy

Basel Action Network (BAN)
www.ban.org
Advocacy organization focused on responsible recycling of electronic waste, with a particular emphasis on preventing the export of waste to developing countries. Created the e-Stewards certification for the responsible recycling of electronics.

California Product Stewardship Council (CPSC)
http://calpsc.org
California-focused EPR advocate whose influence is felt throughout the country.

Call2Recycle
www.call2recycle.org
Product stewardship organization focused on responsible recycling of batteries.

Closed Loop Fund (CLF)
www.closedloopfund.com
A $100M social impact fund that focuses on improving recycling infrastructure in the United States. Strong corporate partnerships.

Cradle to Cradle Products Innovation Institute

www.c2ccertified.org
Certification NGO that administers the Cradle to Cradle product standard. The standard provides designers and manufacturers with criteria and requirements for improving the quality and sustainability of products.

Electronics TakeBack Coalition

www.electronicstakeback.com/home/
Advocate of holding retailers and manufacturers responsible for recycling electronics.

Ellen MacArthur Foundation

www.ellenmacarthurfoundation.org
UK-based foundation focused on fostering the development of circular economies worldwide. Strong focus on partnerships with corporations and startups.

Green Electronics Council (GEC)

http://greenelectronicscouncil.org
Standard setting organization. Manages the EPEAT certification, which is considered by many to be the global standard for the procurement of green electronics.

Product Stewardship Institute (PSI)

www.productstewardship.us
National advocate for EPR laws and voluntary programs. Deep relationships with state and local governments.

Recycle Across America

www.recycleacrossamerica.org
NGO dedicated to increasing recycling rates by making it easier to recycle, primarily through standardized approaches to labeling.

Sustainable Electronics Recycling International (SERI)

https://sustainableelectronics.org
Standard setting organization that created and manages the R2 certification for the responsible reuse, repair and recycling of electronic products.

US Chamber of Commerce Foundation Corporate Citizenship Center

www.uschamberfoundation.org/corporate-citizenship-center
Increasingly important voice on issues such as the circular economy. Information resource and conference host.

Conservation

National Audubon Society

www.audubon.org
Global conservation advocacy organization focused on preserving and improving habitat for birds and other wildlife. Very active local chapters.

National Fish and Wildlife Foundation (NFWF)

www.nfwf.org
Conservation organization created by the US Congress in 1984 to preserve lands to benefit fish and wildlife. One of the largest conservation grantmakers in the world. Growing interest in partnering with corporations.

The Nature Conservancy (TNC)

www.nature.org
Global conservation organization with interests in habitat, climate change and other related environmental issues. Large landowner. Non-confrontational and collaborative in its approach.

Rainforest Alliance

www.rainforest-alliance.org

Global NGO that works to conserve biodiversity and ensure sustainable livelihoods by transforming land use practices, business practices and consumer behavior. Founded in 1987, with over 35,000 members worldwide. Owns and operates the Rainforest Alliance certification program for products that meet their standards.

Trust for Public Land (TPL)

www.tpl.org

Conservation organization whose purpose is preserving and enhancing natural environments for people. Extensive partnerships in both rural and urban areas to create and preserve parks. Considerable in-house real estate expertise.

World Wildlife Fund (WWF)

wwf.panda.org

Multi-dimensional conservation organization that began with a focus on wildlife preservation over fifty years ago. Has developed a solid reputation as a practical problem solver on issues such as climate change through their WWF Climate Savers initiative. Strong emphasis on partnerships.

Media Organizations and Conveners

Ensia

http://ensia.com

Academically oriented media organization focused on sustainability. Excellent resource for digging into the details of complex problems.

Environmental Leader

www.environmentalleader.com

Heavily read daily trade publication that aims to keep corporate executives informed about energy, environmental and sustainability news. Published by Business Sector Media LLC.

GreenBiz Group, Inc.

www.greenbiz.com

Media entity and convener focused on green business. Hosts many conferences and webinars every year. Provides top-notch networking and learning opportunities for sustainability professionals in every type of organization and at every career stage. Runs the GreenBiz website, an excellent resource for information on the intersection of business and sustainability.

Grist

http://grist.org

One of the original environmental media outlets of the digital era. Continues to use a provocative approach in its reporting.

Mother Nature Network

www.mnn.com

General interest environmental media company. Cofounded by advertising industry veteran Joel Babbit and legendary musician and tree farmer Chuck Leavell. Very nice blend of global, national and local content.

Sustainable Brands

www.sustainablebrands.com

Information resource and convener of conferences worldwide that are among the most well attended. Excellent resource, particularly for those who operate on the branding side of the business.

Treehugger

www.treehugger.com
General interest sustainability web site with a focus on green living.

TriplePundit

www.triplepundit.com
The "Triple" stands for People, Planet, Profit. A B Corp media platform with an excellent eye for sustainability trends.

Industry-Specific Associations and Organizations

American Wind Energy Association (AWEA)

www.awea.org
National trade association for the wind industry in the U.S.

Association of Plastic Recyclers (APR)

www.plasticsrecycling.org
National trade association for the recycled plastics industry in the U.S.

Electronic Industry Citizenship Coalition (EICC)

www.eiccoalition.org
Global coalition of companies dedicated to promoting responsibility in the electronics supply chain.

Forest Stewardship Council (FSC)

https://us.fsc.org/en-us
Global, membership-based standard setting organization focused on responsible forest management.

GRESB

www.gresb.com

Industry-driven organization based in the Netherlands committed to assessing the ESG performance of real estate assets globally.

Health Care Without Harm

https://noharm.org

International coalition of health care institutions and other NGOs working to advance environmental responsibility in healthcare.

Institute of Scrap Recycling Industries (ISRI)

www.isri.org

Member-led trade association for the scrap industry.

Practice Greenhealth

https://practicegreenhealth.org

Membership-based organization whose mission is to foster a more sustainable healthcare industry.

Retail Industry Leaders Association (RILA)

www.rila.org/sustainability/Pages/SustainabilityHome. aspx

Trade association for the retail industry. Operates a very active sustainability program for its members.

Solar Energy Industries Association (SEIA)

www.seia.org

National trade association for the solar energy industry in the U.S.

Sustainable Agriculture Network (SAN)

http://san.ag/web/

Coalition of global conservation NGOs that promotes environmental and social sustainability in agriculture through the development of standards for best practices, and certification and training for rural farmers globally.

Sustainable Apparel Coalition (SAC)

http://apparelcoalition.org
Collaborative, industry-based organization that advances sustainability in the apparel industry by developing and implementing pre-competitive approaches to measuring sustainability performance. The primary mechanism for doing this work is a measurement and evaluation tool called the Higg Index. Named after the 18th century haberdasher, Hieronymus D. Higg. Not really.

Sustainable Forestry Initiative (SFI)

www.sfiprogram.org
Independent standard setting organization dedicated to promoting sustainable forest management.

Sustainable Packaging Coalition (SPC)

www.sustainablepackaging.org
Industry working group dedicated to improving the environmental sustainability of packaging. SPC is a project of the non-profit organization GreenBlue.

US Renewable Energy Association (USREA)

http://usrea.org
Membership-based trade association that promotes renewable energy in the U.S.

Conferences

Here's a list of most of the conferences you'll come across in sustainability and CSR. I say "most" because there's always another one out there that I've never heard of.

AASHE Conference

What is it? Large networking and learning event for sustainability professionals in academia, faculty and students. Approximately 2,000 attendees.

Where is it? Location varies. Annual, in fall.

ACEEE National Conference on Energy Efficiency as a Resource

What is it? Large event focused on examining energy efficiency as a strategic and critical utility system resource. Well attended by a diverse array of participants engaged in energy efficiency.

Where is it? Location varies. Biennial, in the odd years, in September.

American Water Works Association Annual Conference and Exposition

What is it? Large international networking and educational conference on water sector issues. Attended by thousands. Heavy vendor presence.

Where is it? Location varies. Annual, in June.

AWEA WINDPOWER

What is it? Large networking and educational conference for the wind energy industry. Heavily attended. Large vendor presence.

Where is it? Location varies. Annual, in spring.

Behavior, Energy, & Climate Conference (BECC)

What is it? Large conference focused on building understanding of individual and organizational behavior and decision-making related to energy usage and climate change. Convened by the Berkeley Energy and Climate Institute, University of California, Precourt Energy Efficiency Center, Stanford University and the American Council for an Energy Efficient Economy. Nearly 700 participants from utilities, NGOs, academia and the energy efficiency industry.

Where is it? Location and timing vary.

Boston College Center for Corporate Citizenship Conference

What is it? Medium-sized networking and learning event for working CSR professionals only. Number of attendees is in the hundreds.

Where is it? Location varies. Annual, typically in March/April.

BSR Conference

What is it? Large, marquis CSR event with most attendees serving in some management role in an organization.

Where is it? Rotates between New York in the even years and California in the odd years. Annual, in October/November.

California Resource Recovery Association Annual Conference

What is it? California-focused resource management event, primarily for professionals in government involved in waste management and recycling. Approximately 500 attendees.

Where is it? Location varies in California. Annual, in August.

Ceres Conference

What is it? Signature sustainability event with an emphasis on SRI. Attendance is typically around 600 and has approached 1,000 in some years.

Where is it? Rotates between Boston in the even years and the Bay Area in California in the odd years. Annual, in April/May.

CE100 Annual Summit

What is it? Executive-level, one-day event hosted by the Ellen MacArthur Foundation that is focused on advancing the circular economy. Medium-sized event that is growing.

Where is it? London. Annual, in early summer.

CleanMed

What is it? Large educational and networking event for environmental professionals in the healthcare field. Over 1,000 attendees.

Where is it? Location varies. Annual, in May.

Climate Leadership Conference

What is it? Medium-sized educational and networking event for practitioners and executives working on climate change issues. Hosted by C2ES and The Climate Registry and sponsored by the US EPA. Diverse audience, with approximately 50% from the corporate sector, 25%

from government and 25% from academia and NGOs. Approximately 400 attendees.

Where is it? Location varies. Annual in February/March.

Climate Strategies Forum

What is it? Educational event primarily for climate change officers pursuing credits for a certification program operated by ACCO.

Where is it? Rotates between East and West coasts. Location and timing vary. Twice/year.

E-Scrap

What is it? Large networking and educational event for the electronics recycling industry. Over 1,000 attendees. Heavy vendor presence.

Where is it? Location varies. Annual, in September/October.

Fortune Brainstorm E: Energy, Technology, and Sustainability

What is it? High-level event that replaced the earlier Fortune Brainstorm Green series that took place annually in Laguna Niguel, California. The newer Brainstorm E started in 2015 and is similar to the former Brainstorm Green in many respects - a heady mix of startups and C-suite executives with an emphasis on networking.

Where is it? Location and time vary. Annual.

GreenBiz

What is it? Signature networking and educational event for sustainability professionals worldwide. Framed around the annual release of the State of Green Business report, GreenBiz's annual assessment of performance and trends in sustainability.

Where is it? Phoenix. Annual, in February.

Greenbuild

What is it? The premier conference and expo in the green building movement. Hosted by USGBC. Large event attended by thousands.

Where is it? Location varies. Annual, in October/ November.

Impact Capitalism Train Stop Tour

What is it? Traveling tour in select cities dedicated to promoting ideas and generating discussion on impact investing. Hosted by the San Francisco-based Big Path Capital, a certified B Corp.

Where is it? Various cities in the U.S. Timing varies.

MIT Sustainability Summit

What is it? Smaller, multi-disciplinary gathering of professionals, academics and students. Excellent forum for in-depth discussions on innovation in sustainability. Typically several hundred attendees.

Where is it? MIT Campus in Cambridge, MA. Annual, in April.

Net Impact Conference

What is it? Premier networking and career-oriented event in sustainability and CSR. Focused on students and practitioners early in their careers, but well attended by professionals at every career stage. Number of attendees is in the thousands.

Where is it? Location varies. Annual, in November.

Plastics Recycling Conference

What is it? Large networking and educational event for the plastics recycling industry. Well attended by professionals in all aspects of plastics recycling, including reclaimers, manufacturers, retailers, government and sustainability practitioners. Heavy vendor presence. Well over 1,000 attendees typically in attendance.

Where is it? Location varies. Annual, spring/summer.

Renewable Energy Markets

What is it? Networking and educational conference for people interested in promoting clean energy. Well attended by a highly diverse audience, including utilities, NGOs, government and renewable energy industry leaders.

Where is it? Location varies. Annual, in fall.

Resource Recycling Conference

What is it? Large networking and educational event for the recycling industry. Heavily attended by professionals working in the waste and recycling industries. Heavy vendor presence. Well over 1,000 attendees typically in attendance.

Where is it? Location varies. Annual, in late summer.

Responsible Business Summit USA

What is it? Smaller networking and educational event hosted by Ethical Corporation that returned to the U.S. in 2016. Mirrors the larger event held annually by Ethical Corp in Europe. Attended by sustainability and CSR executives and practitioners and numbers in the hundreds.

Where is it? New York.

Retail Sustainability & Environmental Compliance Conference (RSECC)

What is it? Well-attended networking and educational event hosted by RILA that brings together leaders and practitioners involved in sustainability and environmental compliance in the retail industry. Approximately 500 attendees and growing every year.

Where is it? Location varies. Annual, in September.

SFI Annual Conference

What is it? Medium-sized conference for professionals engaged in activities related to the SFI certification. Approximately 300 attendees.

Where is it? Location varies. Annual, in September/October.

Shared Value Leadership Summit

What is it? Gathering of leaders interested in advancing ideas and strategies associated with the concept of Shared Value. Attended by approximately 400 people in person, over 12,000 online.

Where is it? New York. Annual, in May.

Social Capital Markets Conference (SOCAP)

What is it? Networking and educational conference focused on increasing the flow of capital toward social good. Convened by MissionHUB LLC, a certified B Corp. Attended primarily by impact investors and social entrepreneurs.

Where is it? San Francisco. Annual, in September.

Solar Power International

What is it? Largest solar energy industry trade show in North America. Over 15,000 attendees. Heavy vendor presence.

Where is it? Location varies. Annual, in September/October.

Supply Chain Conference

What is it? Large networking and educational conference on supply chain management hosted by the Trading Partner Alliance, a collaborative effort of the Grocery Manufacturers Association (GMA) and the Food Marketing Institute (FMI). Well over 1,000 attendees from retailers, manufacturers, brand owners and service providers.

Where is it? Location varies. Annual, in February.

Sustainable Brands

What is it? Large, signature event for sustainability and CSR professionals at all career stages and disciplines. Excellent networking event and a good way to keep up on the latest trends, particularly as it relates to branding.

Where is it? Locations vary. Multiple events around the world throughout the year. The U.S. conference is held in early summer.

Sustainatopia

What is it? Networking and educational event for sustainability and CSR professionals with conference tracks on a variety of topics.

Where is it? Location varies. Once/twice per year, timing varies.

Sustpack

What is it? Networking and educational conference focused on sustainable packaging solutions. Well attended by packaging professionals and hosted by Smithers Pira and the Sustainable Packaging Coalition. Past conferences have had approximately 500 attendees.

Where is it? Location varies. Annual, in March/April.

SXSW Eco

What is it? Collaborative conference that fosters dialogue on sustainability innovation with people from a broad range of perspectives and disciplines. Heavily attended and growing rapidly in numbers and influence. It's where the cool kids hang out.

Where is it? Austin, TX. Annual, in October.

US Chamber of Commerce Foundation Sustainability Forum

What is it? Networking and educational forum focused on business-centered approaches to sustainability.
Where is it? Washington, D.C. Annual, in spring.

Verge

What is it? Global event series hosted by GreenBiz focused on technologies and systems to accelerate sustainability. Known for advancing cutting edge ideas. In addition to the main annual event, hosts other technology and region-specific events.
Where is it? Usually in Northern California. Annual, in September/October.

Waste Expo

What is it? Professional development and educational conference for waste, recycling and organics professionals. Number of attendees is in the thousands. Large vendor presence.
Where is it? Las Vegas. Annual, in June.

People: 100 under 100

Here you'll find a partial list of who's who in sustainability and CSR. Use it to network or create a fantasy league on everyone's Twitter feed or LinkedIn posts. Apologies to the centenarians out there for the blatant ageism, but I had to cut things off somewhere.

To be clear, there is absolutely nothing objective about this list. Every profession has its up and comers as well as those who have been around and have proven to be the best at what they do. Talent that makes your head spin. But if you're looking for a truly objective Top 100 list of the best and the brightest, good luck finding one, because it doesn't exist.

The sustainability profession is a massive spider's web of connections and this list is a starter's kit for figuring out what that network looks like. No more, no less. If you're on the list it's because you have accomplished something and, more importantly, have a reputation for being kind and generous with your time, particularly to people who are trying to find their way in the profession. I know there are more than 100 of you out there that meet these criteria, but really, who actually cares about being on this list anyway, right? Consider it a good start in understanding who you'll run into at conferences and on the major sustainability media outlets.

Because people move around, information is reliable (sort of) and not guaranteed.

Kathy Abusow

President and CEO of Sustainable Forestry Initiative. Kathy has done amazing work to build the profile and credibility of the SFI certification, which has been an enormous and difficult job.

Candace Taylor Anderson

@cmtanderson

Director of Sustainability at Belk Corporation, a large privately held retailer with a growing sustainability and CSR platform. Candace is a savvy and entrepreneurial leader with a nice blend of public and private sector experience.

Tod Arbogast

@Tod_Arbogast

VP of Sustainability and Corporate Responsibility at Avon. Served on the board of Net Impact for many years and is someone who is very committed to helping others in the profession.

John Atcheson

@johnatcheson

Cofounder and CEO of Stuffstr, an early stage circular economy B Corp startup that may just change the way we manage the things in our lives. Tech veteran of several media-related startups and early peer-to-peer car sharing services.

Jonathan Atwood

@JonathanpAtwood

CSO of Unilever, a company that is redefining what it means to be a sustainable business.

Christine Bader

@christinebader

Director of Social Responsibility at Amazon. Author, strategist and a great speaker. Author of *The Evolution of a Corporate Idealist*. One of the many top-flight people to join Amazon recently.

Fred Bedore

@fsbedore

Sustainability strategist and leader at Walmart. Fred has a keen eye for how to maximize business opportunity through sustainability. Key player at a company with enormous influence.

Libby Bernick

@LBernick

Senior VP at the consulting firm Trucost. Libby frequently writes and speaks on sustainability in business and is a leading expert on valuing natural capital.

Michael Bloomberg

@MikeBloomberg

Former Mayor of New York City, current SASB board chair, energetic activist. Super rich guy who puts his money where his mouth is on issues like climate change. Smartest thing he ever did, after figuring out how to make a ton of money, was to hire Ron Gonen to work in his administration.

Sheila Bonini

@boniniwood

CEO of the Sustainability Consortium. Formerly co-led the sustainability practice at McKinsey & Company. Sheila has been involved in a number of sustainability collaborations over the years and knows her stuff.

Mark Buckley

VP of Environmental Affairs at Staples where he's been leading a number of impressive initiatives for years. He has a bachelor's degree in biology, so what's not to like?

Robert Bullard

@DrBobBullard

A true leader whose name is synonymous with environmental justice, Robert has been very influential in how we need to address the impacts and costs of environmental damage inflicted on disadvantaged communities.

Ann Calamai

@AnnCalamai

Director of Sustainability at Optoro, an interesting company in the reverse logistics industry. Ann has a nice mix of experience, including working in renewables, a stint at the US EPA and now a promising circular economy startup.

Henk Campher

@AngryAfrican

Person with the most ironic twitter handle. Yes, Henk is African, but I've never met a more optimistic person. Henk is an excellent strategist with a very deep personal commitment to improving the world. He just *seems* angry sometimes.

Majora Carter

@majoracarter

Sustainability and environmental justice advocate and consultant with an emphasis on improving urban communities. Outstanding speaker and innovator.

Scott Cassel

Founder and CEO of the Product Stewardship Institute and harmonica player. Ask him to play something for you and there's a good chance he'll do it if he has a harmonica handy.

Aimee Christensen

@AimeeGlobal

Founder and Executive Director at Sun Valley Institute for Resilience as well as her own global sustainability consulting firm. Accomplished leader on climate change and renewable energy. Possesses a high level of expertise on the topic of resilience.

Marcus Chung

@marcuschung

VP of CSR at The Children's Place. Very knowledgeable about human rights in the apparel supply chain and tireless advocate on behalf of his alma mater, Wesleyan University. Great source for restaurant recommendations in the Bay Area.

Laura Clise

@lauraclise

ENERGY! The beauty of Laura's career is that she is one of the best at paying attention to the full suite of social and environmental issues we need to be minding to comprehensively pursue sustainability. She is tireless. Meaning she never gets tired. Seriously.

David Connor

@davidcoethica

Sustainability and CSR strategist. Great independent thinker with a talent for pricking the corporate conscience in a way that gets results.

Anisa Kamadoli Costa

@AnisaNYC

CSO at Tiffany & Co. Internationally respected CSR leader who knows a thing or two about the mining industry and sustainability.

Aron Cramer

@aroncramer

President and CEO of BSR. Great person leading a great organization. Very influential, particularly on human rights.

Erin Decker

@erindecker

Former head of sustainability at Salesforce, where she drove impressive change, with an emphasis on renewables. Currently developing new business within the renewable energy sector. One of the many excellent graduates of The Presidio's Sustainable Management MBA program.

Leonardo DiCaprio

@LeoDiCaprio

An actor who's been in some movies and has a serious passion for environmental issues, particularly climate change. An up and comer to keep your eye on. Make sure to introduce yourself and say hello if you see him at a conference.

TJ DiCaprio

@TJDiCaprio

Often credited with being the brains behind Microsoft's innovative internal carbon pricing scheme. It's an impressive effort in corporate sustainability that's being replicated elsewhere. Not related to Leo DiCaprio (as far as we know).

Stephen Donofrio

@StephenDonofrio
Former CDP executive, now an independent strategist with a focus on climate change and business. Stephen knows this space inside and out.

Kevin Dooley

@KDooley_ASU
Professor at Arizona State University and one of the original people involved in forming the Sustainability Consortium. He's still with the Consortium and is super smart on supply chain sustainability.

Cindy Drucker

@CindyDrucker
EVP of the Social Impact practice at Weber Shandwick, a global PR firm. Cindy is somewhat of a unicorn, in that she has experience in the for-profit, non-profit and government sectors (advanced degree from Harvard's JFK School of Government).

Anne Finucane

@AnneFinucane
Power broker at Bank of America who knows her stuff on sustainable investment and social issues like poverty and gender equality. You likely won't run into Anne at a sustainability conference, but make no mistake, she makes things happen in the banking industry.

Gil Friend

@gfriend
Currently the CSO for the city of Palo Alto in California, Gil has been working on sustainability for years. A highly respected practitioner who knows how to push the right buttons. Also rumored to have a black belt in Aikido, so I do whatever he tells me to do.

Jennifer Gerholdt

@JGerholdt

Heads up the Environment Program for the US Chamber of Commerce Foundation Corporate Citizenship Center. The Center is an increasingly important voice on circular economy issues.

Kathy Gerwig

@KathyGerwig

Head of sustainability at Kaiser Permanente, the clear leader in the healthcare community on issues like climate change and toxins in the environment. Every healthcare leader needs to sit down with Kathy for a few minutes to learn why climate change is so important to public health.

Ron Gonen

Cofounder and CEO of the innovative social investment shop, The Closed Loop Fund. Former head of helping people clean up after themselves sustainably for the City of New York under Mayor Michael Bloomberg. Founder of Recyclebank. As you've noticed, he likes to start things. Important things. And they typically do well.

Nina Goodrich

@ninagoodrich

Director of the Sustainable Packaging Coalition. One of the leading experts on sustainable packaging with a bachelor's degree in biology, so what's not to like?

Aida Greenbury

@AidaGreenbury

Leads sustainability and stakeholder outreach for Asia Pulp & Paper Group, the third largest pulp and paper producer in the world. Very active on spearheading change in a resource-intensive industry.

Brigitte Griswold

@bmgriswold

Director of Youth Programs at The Nature Conservancy. Brigitte has been doing fantastic work to engage young people on conservation and environmental issues for over a decade. TNC is lucky to have her on board.

Marc Gunther

@MarcGunther

The best sustainability journalist on the planet. Recently moved over to another beat to focus more on the world of philanthropy, but, like Michael Corleone, we seem to keep dragging him back in.

Kevin Hagen

@kevinhagen

CSR Director at Iron Mountain. Kevin used to head up sustainability for REI and more recently has been building an impressive program at Iron Mountain, a company you may think you know, but has a much bigger influence than you might suspect.

Amy Hargroves

@amyhargroves

Director of CSR and Sustainability at Sprint. Longtime wireless industry veteran with a great understanding of the intersection of business and sustainability.

Paul Hawken

@PaulHawken

His bio says he's an environmentalist, entrepreneur, journalist and author. Yes, yes, yes and yes. In addition, he's a dogged activist that insists on pushing to achieve the seemingly impossible. This is a very good thing and something we need.

Eunice Heath

@euniceheath5

Global Director of Sustainability at Dow Chemical with a particular emphasis on leading the company's engagement with students on sustainability innovation. A much needed voice on the importance of sustainability in STEM education.

Kate Heiny

@kateheiny

Target Corporation's first real sustainability executive who initiated some excellent partnerships while in that role, most notably an effort focused on sustainability in beauty and personal care products with longtime rival Walmart (Rob Kaplan was her counterpart). Currently heading up sustainability for the apparel company C&A in Brussels (Belgium, not Wisconsin).

Garth Hickle

Well known in product stewardship circles, Garth is a highly respected expert on circular economy government policy. Check him out. He knows what he's talking about.

Aaron Hurst

@Aaron_Hurst

Wrote a book on the Purpose Economy. Serial social entrepreneur. Anytime Aaron is speaking at a conference, find yourself a chair and enjoy. He's a great speaker - very entertaining and thought provoking. He talks very fast, so pay attention.

Lisa Jackson

@lisapjackson

Former Administrator of the US EPA, head of environment and sustainability at Apple, which has made significant advancements in sustainability since her arrival.

Hannah Jones

@hjones_nike

Longtime head of sustainable innovation at Nike. Joined Nike at a difficult time in the company's history and, over time, has built and sustained an excellent program with staying power.

Van Jones

@VanJones68

Longtime political strategist and activist, started getting into environmental issues in the mid 2000's. Excellent at challenging the status quo and deftly engaging with people who hold opposing views. A welcome voice in sustainability. Don't miss him if he's speaking at a conference near you.

Cecily Joseph

@CecilyJosephCR

VP of Corporate Responsibility at Symantec and board member at Net Impact. Also teaches at the Presidio Graduate School every now and then. Yes, she's very busy.

Samantha Joseph

First sustainability director at Iron Mountain who successfully pitched and built their program from scratch. Handed the reins to another highly respected pro, Kevin Hagen.

Timothy Juliani

@timjuliani

Heads up strategy and partnerships at C2ES. Excellent collaborator and relationship builder.

Rob Kaplan

@robbyk

Cofounder and Managing Director of The Closed Loop Fund. Rob led a number of great initiatives at Walmart, which ultimately led to his current work at The Closed Loop Fund. Very creative thinker and voted Most Likely to Dream Up The Next Big Thing.

Michael Kobori

@KoboriGrillsCSR

VP of Social and Environmental Sustainability at Levi Strauss & Co. Excellent, well-rounded leader with a solid blend of environmental and human rights experience. Doing a great job of advancing circular economy principles within a large apparel company.

Mark Kramer

Big Thinker on achieving social change through business. Co-creator of the Shared Value strategy with Michael Porter.

Randall Krantz

@randallkrantz

Classic high-impact, low-profile player in the game. A number of years ago, Randall led initiatives on climate change and the circular economy (among other things) at the World Economic Forum. He has an innate sense of how to build partnerships and has had a lot more influence than he or any of us really knows.

Daniel Kreeger

@madscientist826

Cofounder, Executive Director and Mad Scientist of the Association of Climate Change Officers. Yes, that's his title.

Cary Krosinsky

@ckrosinsky

Knows more about sustainable investing than most of us will learn in several lifetimes. Does he have strong opinions? YES!

Bob Langert

@BobLangert

Former VP of Sustainability at McDonald's and currently an Editor at Large at GreenBiz. Bob has been in the business a long time and has been through some of the toughest issues and battles. If you want to get past the BS and politically correct views on sustainability, look him up. Outstanding independent thinker who will tell you how it is.

Alex Laskey

@adlaskey

President and founder of Opower, an energy efficiency technology company. A reformed policy wonk, Alex is one of the pioneers in merging policy, technology and entrepreneurialism to create a successful technology company that is making a difference on climate change.

Chris Librie

@ChrisLibrie

Sustainability leader at HP. Innovative thinker and all around good guy. At the forefront of some truly excellent work at HP.

Amory Lovins

@AmoryLovins

Chairman and Chief Scientist of the Rocky Mountain Institute. One of the smartest science geeks you'll find in this field and a true leader who has built an amazing organization in RMI.

Adam Lowry

@adam_lowry

Serial social entrepreneur and cofounder of Method, the environmentally friendly cleaning products company that is a leader in the B Corp movement. Adam is a chemical engineer and worked as a climate scientist at the Carnegie Institution, so he's no slouch.

Mindy Lubber

@MindyLubber

President and a founding board member of Ceres, an organization that's been focusing on ESG issues for over 25 years. If anybody tries to tell you that sustainable investing has always been a thing, they're lying. Ceres led the way and Mindy has been there from the very beginning.

Dame Ellen MacArthur

@ellenmacarthur

Retired British sailor and founder of the Ellen MacArthur Foundation, an organization that has quickly become the center of activity on the circular economy. Check out her TED talk if you haven't already.

Joel Makower

@makower

Chairman and Executive Editor of GreenBiz Group, Inc., writer of books and a fantastic storyteller. Probably the most influential person out there in corporate sustainability. He's very influential for a very good reason - he knows his stuff and explains things in ways that people can understand and relate to. Also, puns. Many puns. Accidentally created GreenBiz in his Oakland garage with Pete May while trying to design the world's first negative energy accelerator.

Liz Maw

@lizmaw

CEO of Net Impact since 2004. Liz is a frequent writer and speaker, in addition to her huge responsibilities at Net Impact. How does she do it? Watch her in action and you'll realize there are 30 hours in her day.

William McDonough

@billmcdonough

Coauthor with Dr. Michael Braungart of the book *Cradle to Cradle: Remaking the Way We Make Things.* Arguably the most important thinker on the circular economy. All roads in the circular economy lead to Bill.

Susan McPherson

@susanmcp1

Sustainability strategist that seems to be everywhere. Strong advocate on women's issues, ranging from core human rights issues in the developing world to creating a more hospitable environment for women in startup-land.

Elon Musk

@elonmusk

Mad genius behind Tesla, Hyperloop transportation, insanely creative ideas about space travel and undoubtedly a lot of other things he's keeping to himself in his secret lair at the moment. He truly is trying to improve the world through business. Also, it's rare that you have two real-life business titans (the other being Jeff Bezos) duking it out over things like space supremacy, so enjoy the show while you can.

Monique Oxender

CSO at Keurig Green Mountain, a company that has been at the center of difficult discussions on food packaging in the beverage industry. Keurig Green Mountain has been taking heat on the issue of waste generation, but they are far from the only company that has this challenge in their business model. Kudos to Monique for working to find innovative solutions.

Bob Perciasepe

@zipbob50

Former top executive at the US EPA, currently the President of the Center for Climate and Energy Solutions (formerly the Pew Center on Global Climate Change). Bob possesses an exceptionally detailed understanding of how the Federal policy levers work and how best to use them.

Beatriz Perez

@BeaperezBea

Chief Sustainability Officer at the Coca Cola Company, a particularly tough (yet undoubtedly rewarding) job given all of the attention on water these days.

Paul Polman

@PaulPolman

CEO of Unilever and, while understated in most every way, one of the most inspirational business leaders we have around today.

Michael Porter

@MichaelEPorter

Another Big Thinker on achieving social change through business. Co-creator of the Shared Value strategy with Mark Kramer.

Rahul Raj

@rahulwraj

VP of Marketing at ecobee, the incredibly smart, smart thermostat company. Rahul came from Walmart, where he worked on electronics takeback among other things. Used to do improv and has the best LinkedIn feed out there. Very innovative leader.

Todd Reubold
@treubold
Publisher, director and founder of Ensia, a sustainability-focused media platform. Ensia is a great resource for a wide variety of perspectives on sustainability, science and society and we have Todd to thank for much of it.

Andy Revkin
@Revkin
Longtime environmental journalist and accomplished musician. Writes the Dot Earth blog for the New York Times.

Jean Rogers
CEO and Founder of SASB. Came up with the revolutionary concept that if sustainability is material to a business, there ought to be standards for how we account for that. And maybe, just maybe, FASB is a good model. As CFO's become more focused on improving ESG performance, SASB's work will grow in influence and importance.

Marissa Rosen
@MarissaR1
Director of Social Media at TriplePundit. One of our best BS meters. Excellent journalist with a great Twitter feed.

Georgia Rubenstein
@georube
Sustainability Advisor at Forum for the Future. Eclectic strategist who is particularly good at getting people to explore new ideas and concepts.

Helen Sahi

@HelenSahi

Heads up sustainability at Avery Denison, a multi-billion dollar company that is using its influence to advance sustainability in the packaging industry. Helen has been key to making that happen.

Heidi Sanborn

Tireless and highly effective advocate in California for EPR. And I mean tireless. I have a hard time keeping up with her. She moves fast and talks a lot faster than I do, which is saying something.

William Sarni

@WillSarni

Leading water sustainability expert at Deloitte. Will was working on water issues long before anybody thought it was an issue of much importance for companies. Of course, everybody now knows otherwise. Very active on Twitter and LinkedIn.

Shannon Schuyler

@ShannonSchuyler

Head of Corporate Responsibility at Price Waterhouse Coopers, a large firm that operates a leading sustainability consultancy.

Jigar Shah

@JigarShahDC

Renewable energy expert and solar power advocate. Check out Jigar's Twitter feed to watch him challenge the status quo over and over and over again.

Kathleen Shaver

Director of Sustainability and Risk at Cisco. Heavily involved in the Electronics Industry Citizenship Coalition.

Kathleen is very good at embedding sustainability throughout the business.

Margaret Shield

A well respected EPR and public health advocate. Margaret has had a big hand in the development of a number of visionary EPR efforts on the West Coast.

Adam Siegel

@amsiegs

VP of Sustainability for RILA, one of the two major associations in the retail industry. Adam has been influential in shaping how the retail industry views sustainability, whether it's supply chain performance, compliance or overall strategy.

Aman Singh

@AmanSinghCSR

Awesome human being, great writer and one of the best at challenging conventional thinking without pissing people off. Former journalist, now working for RF|Binder as a CSR strategist.

Dave Stangis

@DaveStangis

Head of CSR and Sustainability at Campbell Soup, and longtime board member and supporter of Net Impact. He's been responsible for pushing the food industry in some very positive directions. Dave has a great Twitter feed that often makes my day.

Beth Stevens

Head of Environmental Affairs at Disney. Excellent work on carbon reduction and a longtime champion of partnerships with conservation organizations.

Mark Tercek

@MarkTercek

President and CEO of The Nature Conservancy. Former Big Shot at Goldman Sachs. Very thoughtful guy who's helped people in the investment community understand that we're all in this together.

Trisa Thompson

@TrisaDelCRO

VP of CSR at Dell, one of the companies at the forefront of putting circular economy principles into action.

Beth Trask

@BethTrask

Executive at the Environmental Defense Fund. EDF has done fantastic work to build partnerships with companies on climate change and Beth has been at the center of much of it.

Sally Uren

@sallyuren

CEO of Forum for the Future. Longtime sustainability pro leading an innovative global NGO.

Julie Urlaub

@TaigaCompany

Founder and Managing Partner of Taiga Company, a sustainability consultancy used by a lot of us. Is there a more optimistic person on the planet? I don't think so.

Ellen Weinreb

@SustainableJobs

If you're looking for a job in sustainability and CSR, you had better know who Ellen is and say hello if you see her. The top talent seeker in this field.

Kyle Wiens

@kwiens

Started and runs iFixit, an organization dedicated to the simple concept that we should be able to fix our own stuff to make it last longer. Some of the big companies who want to sell you more stuff, rather than allow you to fix what you already have, aren't fans.

Freya Williams

@freya1

Author and longtime sustainability leader. Currently the North American CEO of the sustainability strategy and communications firm Futerra. Wrote Green Giants, which is a must read.

Kathrin Winkler

@KathrinRW

Head of CSR and Sustainability at EMC Corporation. Excellent strategic thinker and one of the early leaders in sustainability in the tech industry. Kathrin has not pulled up the ladder behind her. She's known for being generous with her time and helping people find their way in the sustainability world.

Andrew Winston

@AndrewWinston

One of the few people who can legitimately claim the mantle of Business Sustainability Guru. He's an author (*Green to Gold, The Big Pivot, Green Recovery*), strategist, consultant and speaker, with a can't miss Twitter feed on a wide range of topics. He's the one who makes you ask yourself, "Why didn't I think of that?"

Acronyms and Abbreviations

AASHE	Association for the Advancement of Sustainability in Higher Education
ACCO	Association of Climate Change Officers
ACEEE	American Council for an Energy-Efficient Economy
AEE	Advanced Energy Economy
AMI	Advanced Meter Infrastructure
APR	Association of Plastic Recyclers
AWEA	American Wind Energy Association
B Corp	Benefit Corporation
BAN	Basel Action Network
BCI	Better Cotton Initiative
BECC	Behavior, Energy & Climate Conference
BICEP	Business for Innovative Climate and Energy Policy
BSR	Business for Social Responsibility
C2ES	Center for Climate and Energy Solutions
CAA	Clean Air Act

CDP	Carbon Disclosure Project
CLF	Closed Loop Fund
COP21	2015 Paris Climate Conference
CPSC	California Product Stewardship Council
CSO	Chief Sustainability Officer
CSR	Corporate Social Responsibility
CSV	Creating Shared Value
CWA	Clean Water Act
DJSI	Dow Jones Sustainability Index
ECOS	Environmental Council of the States
EDF	Environmental Defense Fund
EEI	Edison Electric Institute
EHSS	Environmental Health Safety and Sustainability
EICC	Electronic Industry Citizenship Coalition
EMS	Energy Management System
EMS	Environmental Management System
EPA	US Environmental Protection Agency
EPD	Environmental Product Declaration
EPEAT	Electronic Product Environmental Assessment Tool
EPR	Extended Producer Responsibility

ESG	Environmental, Social and Governance
FASB	Financial Accounting Standards Board
FSC	Forest Stewardship Council
FT	Fair Trade
G3 and G4	Global Reporting initiative's third and fourth generation of sustainability reporting guidelines
GEC	Green Electronics Council
GEMI	Global Environmental Management Initiative
GHG	Greenhouse Gas
GIIN	Global Impact Investing Network
GIS	Geographic Information System
GMO	Genetically Modified Organism
GRI	Global Reporting Initiative
INCR	Investor Network on Climate Risk
ISO	International Organization for Standardization
ISRI	Institute of Scrap Recycling Industries
KPI	Key Performance Indicator
LCA	Life Cycle Analysis
LEED	Leadership in Energy and Environmental Design

MDG	Millennium Development Goal
MRF	Material Recovery Facility
NAEM	National Association for Environmental Management
NALE	North American Latte Exchange
NCA	Natural Capital Accounting
NCAR	National Center for Atmospheric Research
NFWF	National Fish and Wildlife Foundation
NRDC	Natural Resources Defense Council
NREL	National Renewable Energy Laboratory
NGO	Non Governmental Organization
OECD	Organization for Economic Cooperation and Development
OSHA	US Occupational Safety and Health Administration
PCR	Post Consumer Recycled Plastic
PPA	Power Purchase Agreement
PSI	Product Stewardship Institute
RCRA	Resource Conservation and Recovery Act
REACH	Registration, Evaluation, Authorization and Restriction of Chemicals
REC	Renewable Energy Credit

RILA	Retail Industry Leaders Association
ROHS	Restriction of Hazardous Substances
RMI	Rocky Mountain Institute
RSECC	Retail Sustainability & Environmental Compliance Conference
SAC	Sustainable Apparel Coalition
SASB	Sustainability Accounting Standards Board
SDG	Sustainable Development Goal
SEA	Strategic Environmental Assessment
SEIA	Solar Energy Industries Association
SERI	Sustainable Electronics Recycling International
SFI	Sustainable Forestry Initiative
SMM	Sustainable Materials Management
SOCAP	Social Capital Markets Conference
SPC	Sustainable Packaging Coalition
SRI	Socially Responsible Investing
STEM	Science, Technology, Engineering an Mathematics
TCR	The Climate Registry
TNC	The Nature Conservancy
TPL	Trust for Public Land

TSCA	Toxic Substances Control Act
USGBC	US Green Building Council
USREA	US Renewable Energy Association
WEEE	Waste Electrical and Electronic Equipment
WEF	World Economic Forum
WRI	World Resources Institute
WWF	World Wildlife Fund
WWTP	Wastewater Treatment Plant

Field Notes

Field Notes

Field Notes

Field Notes

Field Notes

About the Author

Leo Raudys has worked in sustainability for over 25 years as a government regulator, corporate environmental leader for a Fortune 100 multinational retailer and as a business development executive for an NGO. He's a strategist and speaker who advises companies, investors and NGOs on regulatory and sustainability strategy and stakeholder relations. Leo teaches corporate environmental management at the University of Minnesota and received degrees in biology, psychology and ecology from the University of Illinois at Chicago and the University of Minnesota Twin Cities. You can find him on LinkedIn and Twitter @LeoRaudys.

Praise for The Cheap Guide

The road from here to sustainability is long, winding and full of unexpected detours. We need good maps, and this is one of the best: a succinct, sometimes sassy, guide to who's who and what's what in the world of CSR and sustainable business, designed to help speed the journey.

— Joel Makower, Chairman and Executive Editor, GreenBiz Group, and co-author, *The New Grand Strategy* (St. Martin's Press, 2016)

Sustainability. CSR. Materiality. Natural capital. Circular Economy. ESG. So many words to describe how companies manage their social and environmental issues and contribute to the larger world. Managers trying to understand this growing field could certainly use a "yellow pages" to chart a course through a complex environment. Leo Raudys' new book, *The Cheap Guide to Sustainability and Corporate Social Responsibility*, gives readers a quick overview of the organizations and people trying to build a thriving world, and the language and ideas that inspire them.

Andrew Winston, corporate sustainability advisor, author of *The Big Pivot*, and co-author of *Green to Gold*

Like the *Industrial Revolution and the Information Age* before it, the "Sustainability Era" is underway and accelerating. The conversation will dominate our lives for generations to come, but is complex and difficult to define.

Leo brings needed clarity and organization in *The Cheap Guide to Sustainability and Corporate Social Responsibility*.

Jeremy Hanson
Global Practice Managing Partner, Financial Officers Practice
Heidrick & Struggles

Made in the USA
Middletown, DE
09 November 2016